POP CULTURE PERSONALITIES

ROAR!

BASEBALL STAR

SHOHEI OHTANI

by Noah Leatherland

BEARPORT PUBLISHING

Roar! Books, an imprint of Bearport Publishing by FlutterBee

Credits
Images are courtesy of Shutterstock.com, unless otherwise stated. Cover & Recurring – vladwel, Teodora ART, morokey, Panda Vector, Mogami Kariya, CC BY-SA 2.0, via Wikimedia Commons, Rvector, Conor P. Fitzgerald. 4–5 – Drazen Zigic. 6–7 – Suzanne Tucker. 8–9 – PeopleImages.com - Yuri A, Jacob Lund. 14–15 – Jeffrey Hayes, CC BY 2.0, via Wikimedia Commons. 16–17 – lev radin. 20–21 – milatas. 22–23 – Noah Sauve, Mogami Kariya, CC BY-SA 2.0, via Wikimedia Commons.

Bearport Publishing Company Product Development Team
Kayla Eggert, Theresa Emminizer, Kim Jones, Allison Juda, Cole Nelson, Naomi Reich, Steve Scheluchin, Tiana Tran

Library of Congress Cataloging-in-Publication Data is available at www.loc.gov or upon request from the publisher.

ISBN: 979-8-89577-831-9 (hardcover)
ISBN: 979-8-89577-839-5 (ebook)

For more information, write to Bearport Publishing, 3500 American Blvd W, Suite 150, Bloomington, MN 55431. Printed in the United States of America.

CONTENTS

POP CULTURE PERSONALITY

Crowds gather to watch him play. Fans scream his name. But who is Shohei Ohtani?

Shohei Ohtani is a baseball player. He is one of the best players of all time.

CHILDHOOD

Shohei was born in Japan on July 5, 1994. His family played a lot of sports.

Shohei's father taught him how to play baseball. Even as a young boy, he was very good at the sport.

HIGH SCHOOL

In high school, Shohei broke the Japanese record for the fastest pitch by an 18-year-old.

He was also a very good swimmer. His coach said he was good enough to swim at the Olympics.

TURNING PRO

Shohei became a professional baseball player after leaving high school. He was **drafted** by the Japanese team Hokkaido Nippon-Ham Fighters in 2012.

In 2016, Shohei Ohtani and his team won the Japan Series championship. He was picked as the league's most valuable player, or MVP.

LOS ANGELES ANGELS

In 2017, Shohei joined the Los Angeles Angels. It was the first U.S. team he ever played for.

Shohei worked very hard. In 2018, he was named the American League's **Rookie** of the Year.

LOS ANGELES DODGERS

In 2023, Shohei switched to another team in Los Angeles. He joined the Dodgers. This was one of the biggest deals in sporting history.

In his first season with them, the Dodgers won the National League. Then, they won the 2024 World Series.

PLAYING STYLE

Shohei is known as a two-way player. This means he can play as both a **pitcher** and **hitter**.

It takes a lot of skill to pitch or bat in Major League Baseball (MLB). Very few baseball players can do both!

MAKING HISTORY

Shohei has set many records. He has scored more home runs in the MLB than any other Japanese player.

He is also the first player ever to hit 50 home runs and steal 50 bases in a single season.

CHARITY WORK

Shohei Ohtani has used his fame to help **charities.** In 2024, he helped raise one million dollars to help people in Japan affected by earthquakes.

Shohei has also helped young sports lovers. He donated baseball gloves to 20,000 schools across Japan.

WHAT IS NEXT?

Shohei Ohtani has worked hard. But has become one of the biggest baseball stars.

Shohei will go down as one of the greatest players of all time. What is your favorite thing about him?

GLOSSARY

charities organizations that help those in need

drafted picked by a professional sports team as a new player

hitter the baseball player at bat

pitcher the baseball player who throws the ball to the batter

rookie a member of a sports team playing their first full season

INDEX